Hot & Spicy

Hot & Spicy

Bounty
Books

First published in Great Britain in 2000 by
Hamlyn, a division of Octopus Publishing
Group Ltd

This edition published in 2007 by Bounty Books, a
division of Octopus Publishing Group Ltd
2–4 Heron Quays, London E14 4JP
Reprinted 2008
An Hachette Livre UK Company

ISBN: 978-0-753716-21-2

A CIP catalogue record for this book is available
from the British Library

Printed and bound in China

Notes

1 Standard level spoon measurements are used in all recipes.

1 tablespoon = one 15 ml spoon
1 teaspoon = one 5 ml spoon

2 Both imperial and metric measurements have been given in all recipes. Use one set of measurements only and not a mixture of both.

3 Measurements for canned food have been given as a standard metric equivalent.

4 Eggs should be medium unless otherwise stated. The Department of Health advises that eggs should not be consumed raw. This book may contain dishes made with lightly cooked eggs. It is prudent for more vulnerable people, such as pregnant and nursing mothers, invalids, the elderly, babies and young children, to avoid uncooked or lightly cooked dishes made with eggs. Once prepared, these dishes should be used immediately.

5 Milk should be full fat unless otherwise stated.

6 Poultry should be cooked thoroughly. To test if poultry is cooked, pierce the flesh through the thickest part with a skewer or fork – the juices should run clear, never pink or red.

7 Fresh herbs should be used unless otherwise stated. If unavailable, use dried herbs as an alternative but halve the quantities stated.

8 Pepper should be freshly ground black pepper unless otherwise stated; season according to taste.

9 Ovens should be preheated to the specified temperature – if using a fan-assisted oven, follow the manufacturer's instructions for adjusting the time and the temperature.

10 Do not re-freeze a dish that has been frozen previously.

11 This book includes dishes made with nuts and nut derivatives. It is advisable for customers with known allergic reactions to nuts and nut derivatives and those who may be potentially vulnerable to these allergies, such as pregnant and nursing mothers, invalids, the elderly, babies and children, to avoid dishes made with nuts and nut oils. It is also prudent to check the labels of pre-prepared ingredients for the possible inclusion of nut derivatives.

12 Vegetarians should look for the 'V' symbol on a cheese to ensure it is made with vegetarian rennet. There are vegetarian forms of Parmesan, feta, Cheddar, Cheshire, red Leicester, dolcelatte and many goats' cheeses, among others.

introduction 6

fire starters 10

Fire up your appetite with a recipe from this choice range of soups, hors d'oeuvres and nibbles, including stuffed chillies, and fiery sauces.

flaming fish dishes 26

Ginger, spring onions, soy sauce, garlic, cumin, coriander and lemon grass are among the flavourings that are blended with chilli and onions to produce a great range of fish cakes, curries and stir-fries.

poultry with gusto 40

Influences as far apart as Indonesia, India, Trinidad, the Deep South of America and Edwardian England have inspired the recipes in this chapter, where chicken and turkey take on a variety of spicy guises.

meat with a kick 54

The dishes here include classic recipes such as Chilli con Carne and other dishes with a Tex-Mex flavour; there are also kebabs made with Spanish chorizo and sausages combined with a sublime mustard mash.

sizzling vegetables 68

This chapter is both vegetarian and vegetable. There are main-dish vegetable curries from India and the Far East while, as accompaniments, potatoes, courgettes, kidney beans and even coleslaw get the hot and spicy treatment.

pasta & pizza 82

The two great Italian favourites get a new look here, with pasta combined with spicy sauces and pizzas spread with pungent toppings. Dishes such as Chinese Beef Cappellini and Tagliatelle with Chilli Balsamic Sauce give an exotic twist to Italian basics.

index 96

contents

introduction

There is no doubt that hot, spicy food is addictive. Once you have a taste for it, dishes cooked without hot spices can taste disappointingly bland. The recipes in this collection cater for all levels of taste, ranging from the mildly spiced Piperade on page 24 to Chillies Stuffed with Curried Crab on page 28, a red alert recipe designed for seasoned chilli fanatics.

In the past, attempts to preserve food often involved generous amounts of pepper and other potent seasonings. Such seasonings were also used to disguise the not too savoury taste of meats and other foods served past their sell-by dates! Although spices can add fragrance, flavour and colour to other foods, some are chosen primarily for their heat and strength: the three most important hot spices being chilli, mustard and pepper (see below). Other sources of heat are listed on page 7. If you find your mouth and throat burning from too much hot spice (chilli is the worst offender) then rice, sliced banana or milk may help a little.

Chillies

These are the most powerful of all the hot spices and should be treated with respect. Chillies are used extensively in the cuisines of hot climates as the hot chillies cause the body to perspire and thus, cool it down. They originated in the Amazon region of South America and in Mexico and were brought back to Spain by Columbus, from where they reached Portugal. When the Portuguese established their trading posts in southern India, they took the chilli with them which is how the chillies' heat first found its way into Indian curry dishes. There are over 300 varieties of chilli, ranging from subtle to incendiary flavours. On the whole, the hottest are the tiny ones (the habañero is the most powerful of all), and the seeds and inner membrane the hottest part. Discard them for a milder flavour. The volatile oils in chillies can sting and cause discomfort, so wear rubber gloves when preparing them and do not touch your eyes. Chillies are sold both fresh and dried. Paprika, which may be hot or mild, hot cayenne pepper, crushed chilli flakes and chilli powder are all prepared from chillies.

Mustard

This is prepared from the seeds of three plants of the cabbage family. These seeds, which may be white, brown or black, are the basis of all prepared mustards, which range in strength from hot and sharp, like English mustard, to the mild, sweet and smooth American mustard. To make a powerful English mustard to serve with roast beef, mix the powder with a little cold water and leave for 10–15 minutes before serving. Mustard loses its pungency with heat, which is why large quantities can be added to sauces without overpowering them. French mustards are sold made up rather than in powder form. Dijon is a smooth, pale yellow mustard with a subtle flavour, of varying strength. Bordeaux is dark brown and aromatic, with a sweet-sour taste. Meaux mustard, also called moutarde à l'ancienne, is grainy and mild.

'Variety's the very
spice of life that gives
it all its flavour.'

William Cowper

Pepper

Black, white and green peppercorns all come from the same plant, Piper nigrum, a climbing vine native to the south of India and first brought to Europe in the fifth century BC. The berries are green before they ripen, when they turn bright red. Black peppercorns are picked unripe and then dried in the sun. White peppercorns are the red berries ripened on the vine, then washed, fermented, dehusked and dried. For maximum flavour, black and white peppercorns should be ground in a peppermill as required rather than bought ready ground. Black pepper has the more rounded, aromatic flavour, but some people like to use white pepper in pale coloured dishes, where black flecks may look out of place. The soft, squashy green peppercorns are also picked before they ripen and are packed in vinegar, brine or water, or they may be air-dried.

Spices, Condiments and Sauces

Allspice: Also called Jamaica pepper, this hard, brown berry tastes of cloves, cinnamon and nutmeg. Used in spice mixtures, marinades and some sweet dishes.
Five spice powder: A Chinese spice mixture made from cinnamon, cloves, fennel, star anise and Szechuan pepper.
Garam masala: An Indian blend of hot and aromatic spices, usually containing coriander seeds, cumin, cinnamon, cardamoms, nutmeg and cloves.
Horseradish sauce: A pungent condiment prepared from grated horseradish root and one of Britain's traditional accompaniments to roast beef. Wasabi, sometimes known as Japanese horseradish, is unrelated to true horseradish.
Salsa cruda: Also known as Wet Chilli Mixture, variations of this uncooked chilli and tomato sauce are found throughout Latin America and the Caribbean.
Sambal oelek: An Indonesian sauce made with crushed chillies, salt and vinegar.
Tabasco sauce: A fiery pepper sauce made in Louisiana, USA, from a type of chilli associated in particular with Creole and Tex-Mex cooking.
Thai green and red curry pastes: Two hot Far Eastern curry pastes, the green and red element depending on the type of chillies used.
Worcestershire sauce: A British adaptation of an Indian recipe, made to a secret formula and dating back to the days of the Raj.

thai red curry paste

1 Put all the ingredients in a food processor or blender and process to a thick paste. Alternatively, you can pound together all the ingredients using a pestle and mortar.

2 Transfer the paste to an airtight container. It can be stored in the refrigerator for up to 3 weeks.

10 large fresh red chillies

2 teaspoons coriander seeds

5 cm (2 inch) piece of galangal or ginger, finely chopped

1 lemon grass stalk, finely chopped

4 garlic cloves, halved

1 shallot, roughly chopped

1 teaspoon lime juice

2 tablespoons groundnut oil

Makes about 100 ml (3½ fl oz)

Preparation time: 15 minutes

spicy peanut dressing

1 Chop the creamed coconut and place it in a small saucepan with the milk. Set over a low heat for about 2 minutes, stirring constantly, until the coconut melts and forms a paste with the milk.

2 Transfer the coconut mixture to a food processor or blender. Add the onion, garlic, peanut butter, sugar, soy sauce, ground cumin and chilli powder and season to taste with salt and pepper. Purée until smooth, then scrape into a small bowl. Cover and set aside until required.

25 g (1 oz) creamed coconut

4 tablespoons milk

½ small onion, roughly chopped

1 garlic clove, crushed

4 tablespoons smooth peanut butter

1 teaspoon soft light brown sugar

2 teaspoons soy sauce

½ teaspoon ground cumin

½ teaspoon chilli powder

salt and pepper

Makes about 175 ml (6 fl oz)

Preparation time: 10 minutes

Cooking time: 2 minutes

salsa cruda

1 In a bowl, mix together the tomatoes, onion, chillies, coriander, lemon juice and sugar with salt to taste. Store in an airtight container and serve as required.

500 g (1 lb) tomatoes, skinned, deseeded and diced

75 g (3 oz) chopped onion

65 g (2½ oz) mild green chillies, peeled, deseeded and diced

½ tablespoon finely chopped coriander leaves

1 tablespoon lemon juice

1 teaspoon sugar

salt

Makes about 500 ml (17 fl oz)

Preparation time: 10 minutes

chilli oil

1 Mix together the olive oil, coriander and chilli and season with sea salt and pepper. Leave to infuse for 1–2 days before use. The oil will keep for months if stored in an airtight container.

100 ml (3½ fl oz) olive oil

1 tablespoon finely chopped coriander leaves

1 small red chilli, deseeded and chopped

sea salt and pepper

Makes 100 ml (3½ fl oz)

Preparation time: 5 minutes, plus infusing

■ Drizzle a little chilli oil over savoury dishes to add extra spice, or simply drizzle a little on some fresh crusty bread for a quick and tasty snack.

chilli bean & pepper soup •

cauliflower, coriander & coconut soup •

mexican soup with avocado salsa •

polenta salad with goats' cheese & chilli oil •

watercress & pomegranate salad •

chillies rellenos •

spicy nachos with cheese •

vegetable samosas •

pakora •

stuffed green peppers •

piperade •

chilli bean dip •

fire
starters

chilli bean & pepper soup

1 Heat the oil in a large saucepan and fry the onion and garlic until soft but not coloured. Stir in the peppers and chillies and fry for a few minutes. Stir in the stock and tomato juice or passata, tomato purée, sun-dried tomato paste, chilli sauce, kidney beans and coriander. Bring to the boil, cover, lower the heat and simmer for 30 minutes.

2 Leave the soup to cool slightly, then purée in a food processor or blender until smooth. Return the soup to the pan and taste and adjust the seasoning, adding a little extra chilli sauce if wanted. Bring to the boil and pour into warmed soup bowls. Stir a little soured cream into each one and garnish with strips of lime rind. Serve with tortilla chips.

■ For an interesting variation, use chipotle chillies – a smoked version of jalapeños. They lose none of their heat through the smoking process.

2 tablespoons sunflower oil

1 large onion, finely chopped

4 garlic cloves, finely chopped

2 red peppers, cored, deseeded and diced

2 red chillies, deseeded and finely chopped

900 ml (1½ pints) vegetable stock

750 ml (1¼ pints) tomato juice or passata

1 tablespoon double-concentrate tomato purée

1 tablespoon sun-dried tomato paste

2 tablespoons sweet chilli sauce, or more to taste

425 g (14 oz) can red kidney beans, drained and rinsed

2 tablespoons finely chopped coriander leaves

75 ml (3 fl oz) soured cream

salt and pepper

rind of 1 lime, cut into strips, to garnish

tortilla chips, to serve

Serves 6

Preparation time: 20 minutes

Cooking time: 40 minutes

14

cauliflower, coriander & coconut soup

1 Put the lemon grass, sliced ginger, lime leaves, coriander stalks and vegetable stock into a saucepan. Bring to the boil, cover and simmer for 30 minutes.

2 Heat the oil in a large saucepan, add the onion, garlic, grated ginger and chilli and fry for 5 minutes, until lightly golden. Add the turmeric and cauliflower and fry for a further 5 minutes.

3 Strain the lemon grass stock and add it to the cauliflower mixture. Stir in the coconut milk and coriander leaves, bring to the boil and simmer very gently for 15–20 minutes, until the cauliflower is cooked through and tender. Add the lemon juice, season to taste with salt and pepper and serve in bowls garnished with a drizzle of sesame oil and a few coriander leaves.

2 lemon grass stalks, roughly chopped

4 slices fresh root ginger

4 kaffir lime leaves, bruised

2 coriander stalks, bruised

900 ml (1½ pints) vegetable stock

2 tablespoons sunflower oil

1 onion, thinly sliced

2 garlic cloves, chopped

1 teaspoon grated fresh root ginger

1 red chilli, deseeded and sliced

1 teaspoon ground turmeric

1 cauliflower, trimmed and divided into small florets

400 g (13 oz) can coconut milk

2 tablespoons finely chopped coriander leaves

1 tablespoon lemon juice

salt and pepper

To Garnish:

sesame oil

coriander leaves

Serves 4
Preparation time: 20 minutes
Cooking time: about 1 hour

2 tablespoons sunflower oil

1 large onion, chopped

2 garlic cloves, crushed

2 teaspoons ground coriander

1 teaspoon ground cumin

1 red pepper, cored, deseeded and diced

2 red chillies, deseeded and chopped

425 g (14 oz) can red kidney beans, drained and rinsed

750 ml (1¼ pints) tomato juice

2 tablespoons chilli sauce, or to taste

25 g (1 oz) tortilla chips, crushed

salt and pepper

extra tortilla chips, to garnish

Avocado Salsa:

1 small ripe avocado

4 spring onions, finely chopped

1 tablespoon lemon juice

1 tablespoon finely chopped coriander leaves

Serves 6	
Preparation time: 20 minutes	
Cooking time: 45 minutes	

1 Heat the oil in a large saucepan, add the onion, garlic, spices, red pepper and chillies and fry gently for 10 minutes. Add the beans, tomato juice and chilli sauce and bring to the boil. Cover and simmer over a low heat for 30 minutes.

2 Meanwhile, make the avocado salsa. Peel, pit and finely dice the avocado and combine with the spring onions, lemon juice and coriander. Season to taste with salt and pepper, cover with clingfilm and set aside until required.

3 Put the soup into a food processor with the tortilla chips and purée until smooth. Return to the pan, season to taste with salt and pepper and heat through. Serve the soup in bowls topped with the avocado salsa and extra tortilla chips.

mexican soup with avocado salsa

1 Heat the water until gently simmering, pour in the polenta flour and beat well until it becomes a smooth paste. Reduce the heat and continue to cook, stirring constantly, for 3–4 minutes, until it thickens. Add the butter, season with salt and pepper and mix well, then place the polenta on a chopping board and spread until it is 2.5 cm (1 inch) thick. Leave to set for 5 minutes.

2 Heat a griddle pan and a grill. Spread or crumble the goats' cheese over the polenta, and cut into fingers about 2.5 x 7 cm (1 x 3 inches).

3 Griddle the radicchio for about 2–3 minutes on each side. Arrange on a serving plate with the rocket or watercress.

4 Place the polenta fingers on the griddle and cook for 7–8 minutes. Put the polenta under the grill for 3 minutes, just to melt the goats' cheese, then arrange it on top of the radicchio, drizzle over the chilli oil and balsamic vinegar and season well with sea salt and pepper before serving, garnished with rocket leaves.

600 ml (1 pint) water

150 g (5 oz) instant polenta flour

25 g (1 oz) butter

250 g (8 oz) rindless creamy goats' cheese

1 small radicchio, quartered

125 g (4 oz) rocket or watercress

3 tablespoons Chilli Oil (see page 9)

1 tablespoon balsamic vinegar

sea salt and pepper

rocket leaves, to garnish

Serves 4

Preparation time: 15 minutes

Cooking time: 15–20 minutes

polenta salad with goats' cheese & chilli oil

1   Break open the pomegranate and carefully remove the seeds, discarding the bitter yellow pith. Place the pomegranate seeds in a large bowl with the watercress.

2   Finely grate the rind from 2 of the oranges and set aside. Segment all the oranges, catching the juices in the bowl with the pomegranate seeds and watercress.

3   In a separate bowl, combine the rosewater, olive oil, raspberry vinegar, pink peppercorns and the reserved grated orange rind. Mix well, and then pour over the salad, season with sea salt flakes and serve.

1 pomegranate

1 bunch of watercress, broken into sprigs

4 oranges

1 teaspoon rosewater

5 tablespoons olive oil

1 tablespoon raspberry vinegar

½ teaspoon drained bottled pink peppercorns in brine

sea salt flakes

Serves 4

Preparation time: 15 minutes

watercress & pomegranate salad

■ This peppery salad is a stunning accompaniment to barbecued meat and game. Some people are allergic to pink peppercorns, so you may wish to substitute green ones instead.

chillies rellenos

1 Cut a small slit in each chilli and remove the seeds, leaving on the stems. Dry well with kitchen paper. Place a stick of cheese inside each chilli. Beat the egg whites until stiff. Lightly beat the egg yolks and fold in the whites. Dip the chillies in the egg mixture, then roll them in the flour to coat evenly.

2 Heat the oil in a deep-fat fryer to 180°C (350°F) or until a cube of bread browns in 30 seconds. Deep-fry the chillies until brown, turning occasionally. Drain on kitchen paper, then place in a shallow flameproof dish and top with chilli sauce and cheese. Place under a hot grill to melt the cheese before serving.

6 large fresh poblano or New Mexico chillies, skinned (see page 28)

175 g (6 oz) Cheddar cheese, cut into 25 g (1 oz) sticks

3 eggs, separated

50 g (2 oz) plain flour

sunflower oil, for deep-frying

To Serve:

a little chilli sauce (see page 19)

50 g (2 oz) Cheddar cheese, grated

Serves 3–6
Preparation time: 20 minutes
Cooking time: 15 minutes

250 g (8 oz) tortilla chips

125 g (4 oz) Cheddar cheese, grated

Chilli Sauce:

2 tablespoons vegetable oil

1 onion, chopped

2 garlic cloves, crushed

4 large tomatoes, skinned, deseeded and chopped

2 jalapeño chillies, deseeded and chopped

pinch of dried oregano

pinch of ground cumin

salt and pepper

To Garnish:

2 spring onions, cut into strips

1 red chilli, deseeded and cut into strips

Serves 4–6
Preparation time: 20 minutes
Cooking time: 25–30 minutes

1 First make the chilli sauce. Heat the oil in a small saucepan and sauté the onion and garlic until soft and golden, stirring occasionally. Add the tomatoes, chillies, oregano and cumin and season to taste with salt and pepper. Bring to the boil, lower the heat and simmer gently for about 15 minutes, or until the sauce is thickened and reduced.

2 Arrange the tortilla chips in a large ovenproof dish and spoon the chilli sauce over the top. Sprinkle with grated Cheddar and cook in a preheated oven, 180°C (350°F), Gas Mark 4, for 10–15 minutes, or until the cheese melts and starts to bubble.

3 Meanwhile, soak the spring onion and chilli strips in very cold water for 5–10 minutes to make them curl. Serve the nachos garnished with spring onion and chilli curls.

spicy nachos with cheese

vegetable samosas

1 First make the pastry. Sift the flour and salt into a bowl. Rub in the ghee or butter until the mixture resembles breadcrumbs. Add the water and knead to a very smooth dough. Cover and chill while preparing the filling.

2 To make the filling, heat the oil in a large saucepan and add the mustard seeds. Leave for a few seconds until they start to pop, then add the onion and fry for 5 minutes, until golden. Add the chillies, turmeric, ginger and salt to taste and fry for 3 minutes; if the mixture starts sticking to the pan, add 1½ teaspoons water and stir well. Add the peas, stir thoroughly and cook for 2 minutes. Add the potatoes and coriander, stir well and cook for 1 minute. Stir in the lemon juice. Allow to cool slightly.

3 Divide the pastry into 8 pieces. Dust with flour and roll each piece into a thin round, then cut each round in half. Carefully fold each half into a cone and brush the seam with water to seal.

4 Fill the cone with a spoonful of filling (do not overfill), dampen the top edge and seal firmly. Heat the oil and deep-fry the samosas until crisp and golden. Serve hot or warm with the mint and yogurt sauce or a cooling raita.

125 g (4 oz) plain flour

¼ teaspoon salt

25 g (1 oz) ghee or butter

2–3 tablespoons water

oil, for deep-frying

Mint and Yogurt Sauce (see page 38), to serve

Filling:

1 tablespoon vegetable oil

1 teaspoon mustard seeds

1 small onion, finely chopped

2 green chillies, minced

¼ teaspoon ground turmeric

1 teaspoon finely chopped fresh root ginger

125 g (4 oz) frozen peas

125 g (4 oz) cooked potatoes, diced

½ tablespoon finely chopped coriander leaves

1 tablespoon lemon juice

salt

Serves 4

Preparation time: 15 minutes, plus cooling and chilling

Cooking time: about 30 minutes

pakora

1 Sift the flour, salt and chilli powder into a bowl. Stir in enough water, about 150 ml (¼ pint), to make a thick batter and beat well until smooth. Leave to stand for about 30 minutes.

2 Stir the chillies and coriander into the batter, then add the vegetable oil. Add the onion rings and coat thickly with batter.

3 Heat the oil in a deep pan, drop in the onion rings and deep-fry until they are crisp and golden. Remove from the pan with a slotted spoon, drain on kitchen paper and keep warm.

4 Dip the spinach leaves into the batter and deep-fry in the same way, adding more oil to the pan if necessary. Repeat the process with the potato slices. Serve hot with a selection of chutneys.

125 g (4 oz) gram (besan) flour

1 teaspoon salt

½ teaspoon chilli powder

2 green chillies, finely chopped

1 tablespoon finely chopped coriander leaves

1 tablespoon vegetable oil, plus extra for deep-frying

2 onions, sliced into rings

8 small spinach leaves, washed

2–3 potatoes, parboiled and sliced

Serves 4

Preparation time: 20 minutes, plus standing

Cooking time: about 30 minutes

■ Gram flour is made from chickpeas and is suitable for people allergic to gluten, a component of wheat products.

1 Place the peppers in a large saucepan and cover with cold water. Bring to the boil, then reduce the heat and simmer gently until the peppers are tender but still firm. Drain and leave to cool.

2 To prepare the stuffing, heat the oil in a large frying pan and add the onion, garlic and chilli. Fry gently over a low heat until the onion is soft and golden brown. Add the minced beef and stir well. Continue cooking over a low heat until well browned. Add the lemon rind and cooked rice. Season to taste with salt, pepper and paprika. Cook gently for 5 minutes and then stir in the chopped chives.

3 Slice the tops off the peppers and scoop out the seeds. Fill with the stuffing and place in a greased baking tin. Surround with the tomatoes and bake in a preheated oven, 180°C (350°F), Gas Mark 4, for about 20 minutes. Garnish with snipped chives and serve hot.

4 large green peppers

4 tomatoes, thinly sliced

salt and pepper

snipped chives, to garnish

Spicy Stuffing:
2 tablespoons vegetable oil

1 small onion, finely chopped

1 garlic clove, crushed

1–2 red chillies, deseeded and finely chopped

125 g (4 oz) minced beef

grated rind of 1 lemon

4 tablespoons cooked rice

pinch of paprika

a few chopped chives

Serves 4
Preparation time: 15 minutes
Cooking time: 45 minutes

stuffed green peppers

1 Heat 6 tablespoons of the oil in a frying pan, add the pepper strips and sauté over a moderate heat until soft, stirring frequently. Add the onions, chilli and garlic and fry gently for 10 minutes, stirring. Add the sugar, tomatoes, bouquet garni and season with salt and pepper. Cook over a low heat for a further 10 minutes, stirring occasionally. Heat the remaining olive oil in a separate pan and heat the slices of ham gently.

2 Pour the beaten eggs into a lightly oiled or greased frying pan and cook for 2–3 minutes over a very low heat without stirring.

3 Discard the bouquet garni, then stir the vegetable mixture into the eggs. Keep stirring until the eggs start to scramble and cook through. Adjust the seasoning to taste. Serve the piperade straight from the pan accompanied by the slices of ham.

piperade

■ Skin tomatoes by cutting a small cross in the base and then placing them in boiling water for about 1 minute. Drain and cool slightly. The skins should then slip off easily.

7 tablespoons olive oil

4 large red peppers, peeled (see page 52), deseeded and cut into thin strips

4 large onions, thinly sliced

1 hot red chilli, thinly sliced

2 garlic cloves, crushed

pinch of sugar

1 kg (2 lb) tomatoes, skinned, deseeded and chopped

1 bouquet garni

6 thick slices ham

6 eggs, lightly beaten

salt and pepper

Serves 6

Preparation time: 15–20 minutes

Cooking time: 25–30 minutes

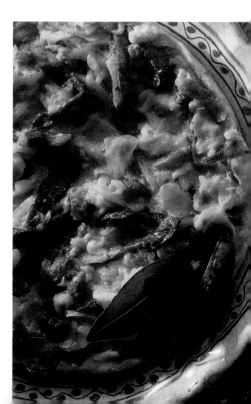

chilli bean dip

1 Put the pepper flesh, half the oil, garlic and chilli in a food processor or blender and process until well chopped. Add the beans and paprika and continue to process until a coarse purée forms. Season to taste with Tabasco and salt and pepper. With the machine running, add the rest of the oil to make a thick paste.

2 Pile the bean purée into a bowl and sprinkle with the chives. Cover and refrigerate until required. Serve with fresh vegetables, corn chips or toasted pitta bread to dunk into the dip.

■ This dip is also very good served spread on bruschetta, like a pâté.

2 large red peppers, skinned (see page 52), halved lengthways and deseeded

2 tablespoons olive oil

2 garlic cloves, crushed

1 red chilli, deseeded and finely chopped

425 g (14 oz) can red kidney beans, drained and rinsed

½ teaspoon paprika

dash of Tabasco sauce

salt and pepper

2 tablespoons snipped chives, to garnish

assorted fresh vegetables, corn chips or toasted pitta bread, to serve

Makes about 400 ml (14 fl oz)
Preparation time: 20 minutes, plus chilling

chillies stuffed with curried crab •

prawns & noodles in spicy broth •

chillied fish •

fish curry •

spicy fish stew •

stir-fried prawns with cumin & chilli •

roasted thai-style prawns •

creole prawns •

spicy baked fish •

spiced fish cakes •

flaming fish dishes

1 To prepare the chillies for stuffing, put them under a preheated hot grill for 8–10 minutes, turning them occasionally, until they have softened and their skins are charred and patched with black. Remove the chillies from the grill and leave to cool, covered with damp kitchen paper. (This will make their skins easier to peel.)

2 Meanwhile, prepare the stuffing. Heat the oil in a saucepan, add the garlic, ginger and spring onions and cook over a gentle heat, stirring occasionally, for 3 minutes, until softened. Stir in the lime leaves, red curry paste and turmeric and cook, stirring, for 2 minutes. Remove the pan from the heat and stir in the flaked crab, lime juice and fish sauce.

3 Peel the chillies, leaving the stalks intact, and make a slit down one side of each chilli from the stalk to the tip. Scrape out and discard the seeds. Stuff the chillies with the curried crab mixture, place them in a single layer in a shallow ovenproof dish and cover with foil. Cook in a preheated oven, 200°C (400°F), Gas Mark 6, for 15 minutes, until they are heated through. Serve immediately.

6 red jalapeño chillies

6 green jalapeño chillies

2 tablespoons vegetable oil

2 garlic cloves, crushed

1 teaspoon grated fresh root ginger

3 spring onions, chopped

2 kaffir lime leaves, very finely chopped

1 tablespoon Thai red curry paste (see page 8)

¼ teaspoon ground turmeric

150 g (5 oz) fresh or canned white crab meat, flaked

1 tablespoon lime juice

2 teaspoons Thai fish sauce

Serves 4–6

Preparation time: about 30 minutes

Cooking time: 30 minutes

chillies stuffed with curried crab

prawns & noodles in spicy broth

1 Put the prawns into a bowl with a pinch of salt. Mix the cornflour to a smooth paste with the cold water, and stir into the prawns.

2 Cook the egg noodles according to the packet instructions in a large saucepan of lightly salted boiling water or until just tender. Drain well and place the noodles in a large, warm serving bowl. Bring the stock to the boil and pour it over the noodles with half of the soy sauce. Keep warm.

3 Heat the oil in a wok and add the shredded spring onions to flavour the oil. Add the prawn mixture and bamboo shoots or mushrooms and spinach. Stir a few times and then add 1½ teaspoons salt, the remaining soy sauce and the sherry. Cook for 1–2 minutes, stirring constantly.

4 Pour the mixture over the noodles and sprinkle with sesame oil. Serve immediately garnished with chopped red chilli and coriander sprigs.

250 g (8 oz) cooked, peeled prawns

1 teaspoon cornflour

1 tablespoon cold water

375 g (12 oz) egg noodles

600 ml (1 pint) chicken stock

2 tablespoons light soy sauce

3 tablespoons vegetable oil

2 spring onions, thinly shredded

125 g (4 oz) bamboo shoots or button mushrooms, thinly sliced

125 g (4 oz) spinach, thinly sliced

2 tablespoons dry sherry

1–2 tablespoons sesame oil

salt

To Garnish:

1 red chilli, chopped

coriander sprigs

Serves 4	
Preparation time: 15 minutes	
Cooking time: 15 minutes	

chillied fish

1 Put the rice, water and salt into a saucepan. Bring to the boil and stir once. Cover and simmer for 15 minutes, or according to the packet instructions, until the rice is tender and all the liquid has been absorbed.

2 While the rice is cooking, combine all the sauce ingredients in a jug and set aside.

3 Coat the fish with flour. Heat the oil in a wok, add the fish and fry for 3 minutes. Remove the fish and reheat the oil, then return the fish to the pan to crisp it. Remove the fish, drain on kitchen paper, then transfer to a warmed serving dish. Pour the chilli sauce into the wok and cook for 2 minutes, then pour over the fish. Serve immediately with the rice.

250 g (8 oz) long-grain rice

300 ml (½ pint) water

½ teaspoon salt

500 g (1 lb) fish fillets, (e.g. cod or plaice), cut into 5 cm (2 inch) slices

flour, for coating

300 ml (½ pint) vegetable oil

Ginger & Chilli Sauce:

2 teaspoons finely chopped fresh root ginger

1 tablespoon chopped spring onion

3 tablespoons dry sherry

1 tablespoon soy sauce

2 teaspoons sugar

1 teaspoon salt

1 tablespoon chilli sauce (ready-made or see page 19)

Serves 4

Preparation time: 10–15 minutes

Cooking time: about 20 minutes

1 Melt the butter in a heavy-based frying pan over a low heat, taking care that it does not brown. Add the onion and garlic and cook gently until softened and golden. Add the curry powder and flour, stir well and cook gently for 2 minutes, stirring. Add the coconut milk and chilli and stir to mix them thoroughly. Simmer gently for 5–10 minutes, until smooth and thickened.

2 Meanwhile, skin the fish fillets with a sharp knife. Discard the skin and arrange the fillets in a large, shallow ovenproof dish. Sprinkle the lime juice over the top.

3 Season the curry sauce to taste with salt and pepper and pour over the fillets. Cover the dish and cook in a preheated oven, 170°C (325°F), Gas Mark 3, for about 12–15 minutes, until the fish is just cooked but still firm. Sprinkle with coriander and serve with boiled rice and mango chutney.

40 g (1½ oz) butter

1 large onion, finely chopped

1 garlic clove, crushed

1 tablespoon curry powder

1 tablespoon flour

400 ml (14 fl oz) coconut milk

1 green chilli, deseeded and chopped

625 g (1¼ lb) white fish fillets

juice of ½ lime

salt and pepper

chopped coriander, to garnish

To Serve:

boiled rice

mango chutney

Serves 4
Preparation time: 10 minutes
Cooking time: 25–30 minutes

fish curry

■ The word 'curry' comes from the southern Indian word 'kari', which means sauce. To save time, you could serve it with warmed naan bread instead of rice.

spicy fish stew

1 Heat the oil in a large heavy-based saucepan and gently sauté the onion, garlic and peppers, stirring occasionally, for about 10–15 minutes, or until tender.

2 Add the tomatoes, ginger, coriander, oregano, lime rind, chilli sauce and dried red chillies. Stir well, then simmer gently over a low heat for 10 minutes.

3 Add the monkfish and fish stock to the pan and bring to the boil. Reduce the heat and simmer gently for 20 minutes.

4 Stir in the scallops and prawns and cook gently for 2 minutes, until they are cooked. Season to taste with salt and pepper and serve garnished with coriander leaves.

3 tablespoons olive oil

1 large onion, chopped

2 garlic cloves, crushed

1 large red pepper, cored, deseeded and chopped

1 large yellow pepper, cored, deseeded and chopped

500 g (1 lb) tomatoes, skinned and chopped

2 tablespoons finely chopped fresh root ginger

1 tablespoon finely chopped coriander leaves

2 teaspoons chopped oregano

grated rind of 1 lime

dash of hot chilli sauce

2–4 dried red chillies, chopped

1.25 kg (2½ lb) monkfish, skinned, boned and cut into chunks

300 ml (½ pint) fish stock

12 fresh scallops, cleaned and halved

250 g (8 oz) raw prawns

salt and pepper

coriander leaves, to garnish

Serves 6

Preparation time: 15 minutes

Cooking time: 45 minutes

■ Scallops are usually sold opened and cleaned, or ask your fishmonger to do it for you.

stir-fried prawns with cumin & chilli

1 Heat the oil in a wok or frying pan until it is hot, then stir-fry the cumin seeds and turmeric for 30 seconds. Add the onion and stir-fry for about 5 minutes, until it starts to brown. Add the pepper, tomatoes, chillies and season to taste with salt. Stir-fry for 2 more minutes.

2 Reduce the heat and add the prawns. Simmer for about 5 minutes, just long enough to make them hot. Do not overcook them or they will become rubbery. Serve immediately, garnished with fennel or coriander sprigs.

■ Cumin goes well with fish, vegetables, pulses and grains. Its delicate but permeating flavour also blends well with ground or fresh coriander.

4 tablespoons sunflower oil

2 tablespoons white cumin seeds

1 teaspoon ground turmeric

1 onion, finely chopped

¼ green pepper, chopped

2 tomatoes, skinned and chopped

1–2 green chillies, finely chopped

750 g (1½ lb) peeled prawns

salt

fennel or coriander sprigs, to garnish

Serves 4

Preparation time: 10 minutes

Cooking time: about 12 minutes

750 g (1½ lb) raw tiger prawns, peeled and deveined

400 ml (14 fl oz) coconut milk

1 tablespoon Thai fish sauce

1 tablespoon light soy sauce

2 garlic cloves, crushed

2.5 cm (1 inch) piece of fresh root ginger, grated

1 tablespoon ground coriander

2 teaspoons ground cumin

1 bunch of fresh coriander, chopped

2 red chillies, deseeded and sliced

2 teaspoons sugar

2 lemon grass stalks, finely sliced

egg noodles, to serve

To Garnish:

chopped coriander leaves

chopped red chilli

Serves 4
Preparation time: 5–10 minutes
Cooking time: 10–12 minutes

1 Place the prawns in a shallow ovenproof dish and set aside. Put all the other ingredients, except the noodles, into a food processor or blender and purée until fairly smooth. Pour the sauce over the prawns and roast in a preheated oven, 200°C (400°F), Gas Mark 6, for 7 minutes, or until the prawns turn pink and are just cooked through. Remove the prawns with a slotted spoon and set aside.

2 Pour the sauce into a small pan and heat for 3–5 minutes to reduce slightly. Pour over the prawns.

3 Serve the prawns on a bed of egg noodles, garnished with coriander and chilli.

roasted thai-style prawns

■ Fish sauce, also known as nam pla, is used in Thai cooking in much the same way as the Chinese use soy sauce. It is available from most large supermarkets and Asian foodstores.

1 tablespoon oil

1 large onion, chopped

1 garlic clove, crushed

2 celery sticks, thinly sliced

375 g (12 oz) tomatoes, skinned, deseeded and chopped

1 green pepper, cored, deseeded and finely chopped

4 tablespoons dry white wine

1 tablespoon tomato purée

500 g (1 lb) peeled, cooked prawns

2–4 drops Tabasco sauce

1 teaspoon Worcestershire sauce

1 tablespoon chopped parsley

salt and pepper

To Garnish:

lemon twists

celery leaves (optional)

To Serve:

rice or pasta

green salad

Serves 6
Preparation time: 10 minutes
Cooking time: 35–40 minutes

1 Heat the oil in a saucepan, add the onion and garlic and fry until lightly browned. Add the celery and cook for 2 minutes.

2 Add the tomatoes and green pepper and season to taste with salt and pepper. Stir in the wine and tomato purée. Bring to the boil and simmer, uncovered, for 20 minutes.

3 Stir in the prawns, Tabasco and Worcestershire sauces. Simmer for 5 minutes, then stir in the parsley. Serve immediately, garnished with lemon twists and celery leaves, if liked. Serve with rice or pasta and a green salad.

creole prawns

spicy baked fish

1 Wash and dry the fish and place in a large dish. Sprinkle with the lime juice and season inside and out with salt and pepper. Leave in a cool place for about 1 hour to marinate.

2 To make the stuffing, put the breadcrumbs into a bowl and mix in the melted butter. Stir in all the remaining stuffing ingredients. Mix well, cover and set aside.

3 To make the topping, heat the oil in a frying pan and add the onion and garlic. Fry gently until the onion is softened. Add the chilli and continue cooking for 2–3 minutes, then stir in the coriander and stock.

4 Remove the fillets from the marinade and sandwich together with the stuffing. Fasten with wooden cocktail sticks. Pour over the oil and any remaining marinade and scatter the topping mix over the fish. Bake in a preheated oven, 180°C (350°F), Gas Mark 4, for 20 minutes. Serve garnished with fried onion rings.

1.5 kg (3 lb) sea bass or bream, cleaned, scaled and filleted

juice of 2 limes

6 tablespoons olive oil

salt and pepper

deep-fried onion rings, to garnish

Stuffing:

125 g (4 oz) fresh breadcrumbs

50 g (2 oz) butter, melted

1 tablespoon finely chopped chives

1 teaspoon finely chopped coriander

1 small green pepper, cored, deseeded and finely chopped

½ onion, grated

grated rind and juice of 1 lime

pinch of grated nutmeg

Topping:

2 tablespoons oil

1 small onion, chopped

1 garlic clove, crushed

1 red chilli, deseeded and chopped

1 tablespoon chopped coriander

4 tablespoons fish stock

Serves 4

Preparation time: 25 minutes, plus marinating

Cooking time: 30 minutes

spiced fish cakes

1 Put the skimmed milk and bay leaf into a saucepan. Add the fish and poach for 10 minutes, turning once. Leave to cool slightly, then drain and chop the fish, reserving the milk.

2 Meanwhile, make the mint and yogurt sauce. Put the yogurt into a small bowl and beat in the spring onions, mint and lemon juice. Cover with clingfilm and chill in the refrigerator until ready to serve.

3 Melt the butter or margarine in a saucepan, add the onion and green pepper and cook over a moderate heat for 3 minutes, stirring once or twice. Stir in the chilli powder and cook for 1 minute. Stir in the flour. Pour on the reserved milk, stirring constantly until the sauce boils. Simmer for 3 minutes. Beat the sauce thoroughly. Remove the pan from the heat, beat in the fish and season with salt. Beat in half of the egg. Leave to cool, then shape into eight flat cakes.

4 Combine the breadcrumbs and peanuts. In another bowl, beat the remaining egg with the milk. Dip the fish cakes into the egg mixture and then into the breadcrumb mixture to coat. Heat the oil in a nonstick frying pan and fry the cakes for about 3–4 minutes on each side.

5 Spoon a little of the sauce on to each plate and serve the fish cakes on top, garnished with the spring onions. Serve the remaining sauce separately.

300 ml (½ pint) skimmed milk

1 bay leaf

500 g (1 lb) coley or other white fish fillets, skinned

25 g (1 oz) butter or margarine

1 small onion, finely chopped

1 green pepper, cored, deseeded and finely chopped

½ teaspoon chilli powder, or to taste

25 g (1 oz) wholemeal flour

1 egg, beaten

4 tablespoons wholemeal breadcrumbs

50 g (2 oz) peanuts, crushed or finely chopped

1 tablespoon milk

2 tablespoons sunflower oil

salt

finely chopped spring onions, to garnish

Mint and Yogurt Sauce:

150 ml (¼ pint) Greek yogurt, chilled

3 spring onions, finely chopped

2 tablespoons chopped mint

1 teaspoon lemon juice

Serves 4

Preparation time: 25 minutes, plus cooling

Cooking time: about 35 minutes

curried chicken salad ●

gado gado with chicken ●

kashmiri chicken ●

chicken jalfrezi ●

trinidadian pilau ●

grilled chicken creole ●

phuket chicken curry ●

devilled chicken ●

spicy pot roast chicken ●

spiced chicken wings & pepper dip ●

red hot turkey sandwich ●

poultry with gusto

curried chicken salad

1 Skin the chicken and remove all the meat from the carcass. Cut the meat into bite-sized pieces and place in a bowl with the grapes. Season to taste with salt and pepper. Tear the salad leaves into bite-sized pieces and arrange to form a bed on a serving platter or on individual plates.

2 Mix together all the dressing ingredients in a small bowl, adding just enough cold water to give a thick pouring consistency.

3 Add the dressing to the chicken mixture and toss gently until combined. Pile the mixture on to the salad leaves and garnish with a few coriander sprigs.

■ Chicken salad recipes are great ways of using up leftover cooked chicken.

1 small whole cooked chicken, about 1.25 kg (2½ lb)

175 g (6 oz) seedless grapes, halved

about 250 g (8 oz) mixed salad leaves (e.g. cos, red oakleaf, lamb's lettuce, rocket, frisée)

salt and pepper

coriander sprigs, to garnish

Dressing:

6 tablespoons mayonnaise

1 tablespoon medium-hot curry paste

1–2 tablespoons mango chutney

Serves 4

Preparation time: 20 minutes

gado gado with chicken

1 Bring a large saucepan of water to the boil, add the carrot, celery and leek matchsticks and blanch for 1–2 minutes. Drain in a colander, refresh under cold running water, then drain again thoroughly. Tip into a bowl.

2 Cut the mangetout in half diagonally. Using a teaspoon, scoop out the seeds from the cucumber and cut the flesh into slices. Add the mangetout, cucumber and bean sprouts to the bowl. Season with salt and pepper. Gently toss together all the vegetables.

3 Arrange the pak choi leaves on a serving platter or individual plates and top with the shredded chicken and the vegetable mixture. Spoon over the dressing. Garnish with chopped coriander.

■ Vegetarians can omit the chicken from this Indonesian salad or replace it with cubed tofu fried in a little oil until golden brown all over.

250 g (8 oz) carrots, cut into matchsticks

175 g (6 oz) celery, cut into matchsticks

175 g (6 oz) leeks, cut into matchsticks

125 g (4 oz) mangetout

½ cucumber, peeled and halved lengthways

175 g (6 oz) bean sprouts

about 175 g (6 oz) pak choi

2 cooked chicken breasts, skinned and shredded

1 quantity Spicy Peanut Dressing (see page 8)

salt and pepper

chopped coriander, to garnish

Serves 4

Preparation time: 30 minutes

Cooking time: 1–2 minutes

kashmiri chicken

1 Melt the ghee or butter in a wok. Add the onions, peppercorns, cardamoms and cinnamon and fry for about 8–10 minutes, stirring occasionally, until the onions are golden. Add the ginger, garlic, chilli powder, paprika and salt and fry for 2 minutes, stirring occasionally.

2 Add the chicken pieces and fry until they are evenly browned. Gradually add the yogurt, stirring constantly. Cover and cook for about 30 minutes, or until the chicken is done. Garnish with lime wedges and parsley and serve with naan bread.

■ Ghee is clarified butter, originally from northern India, from which all the milky solids have been removed, and can be heated to a higher point without burning than unclarified butter. It is available from Asian shops and supermarkets and keeps well.

50 g (2 oz) ghee or butter

3 large onions, thinly sliced

10 peppercorns

10 cardamom pods

5 cm (2 inch) piece of cinnamon stick

5 cm (2 inch) piece of fresh root ginger, chopped

2 garlic cloves, finely chopped

1 teaspoon chilli powder

2 teaspoons paprika

1.5 kg (3 lb) chicken pieces, skinned

250 ml (8 fl oz) natural yogurt

salt

naan bread, to serve

To Garnish:

lime wedges

chopped parsley

Serves 4–6

Preparation time: 10 minutes

Cooking time: about 45 minutes

1 Heat the oil in a large flameproof casserole, add the onion, ginger and garlic and fry over a gentle heat, stirring frequently, for 5 minutes, until softened but not coloured. Add the chillies, garam masala and ground coriander and fry, stirring constantly, for 2–3 minutes to release the aroma of the spices. Add the tomatoes, tomato purée, lemon juice, sugar and ½ teaspoon salt. Stir well to mix, then pour in the stock and bring to the boil over a moderate heat, stirring all the time. Simmer for about 15 minutes, until thickened and reduced.

2 Add the chicken, cover and simmer over a gentle heat, stirring occasionally, for 30 minutes.

3 Add the chopped green pepper and coriander leaves and simmer for a further 10 minutes, or until the chicken is tender when pierced with a skewer or fork. Taste for seasoning, and serve hot, with boiled rice or chapatis, and a selection of raitas and chutneys.

2 tablespoons vegetable oil

1 onion, finely chopped

5 cm (2 inch) piece of fresh root ginger, peeled and crushed

1 garlic clove, crushed

2 small red chillies, very finely chopped

2 teaspoons garam masala

2 teaspoons ground coriander

6 ripe tomatoes, peeled, deseeded and roughly chopped

1 tablespoon tomato purée

2 teaspoons lemon juice

¼ teaspoon sugar

450 ml (¾ pint) chicken stock

1 kg (2 lb) boneless, skinless chicken thighs, cut into bite-sized pieces

1 large green pepper, cored, deseeded and chopped

2 tablespoons chopped coriander

salt

To Serve:

boiled rice or chapatis

selection of raitas and chutneys

Serves 4–6
Preparation time: 20 minutes
Cooking time: about 1 hour

chicken jalfrezi

trinidadian pilau

2 kg (4 lb) chicken, cut into pieces

3 tablespoons groundnut oil

15 g (½ oz) butter

1 onion, finely chopped

2 garlic cloves, crushed

1 red pepper, cored, deseeded and chopped

1 red chilli pepper, deseeded and finely chopped

375 g (12 oz) long-grain rice

2 tomatoes, skinned and chopped

900 ml (1½ pints) chicken stock

a few saffron threads

thyme sprig

Seasoning Mixture:

1 garlic clove

2 allspice berries

1 teaspoon dried mixed herbs

salt and pepper

To Garnish:

50 g (2 oz) chopped roasted peanuts

chopped red chilli

Serves 6	
Preparation time: 10 minutes, plus marinating	
Cooking time: 40 minutes	

1 Put the ingredients for the seasoning mixture in a mortar and pound well with a pestle until the garlic and allspice berries are crushed and blended with the salt, pepper and herbs. Rub the seasoning mixture all over the chicken pieces, cover and leave in the refrigerator for several hours or overnight.

2 Heat the oil and butter in a large frying pan and add the chicken pieces. Fry over a moderate heat, turning several times, until they are golden brown all over, then remove from the pan and keep warm.

3 Add the onion, garlic, red pepper and chilli to the pan and fry over a gentle heat until softened but not browned. Add the rice and turn in the oil until all the grains are coated. Stir in the tomatoes, stock, saffron and thyme. Return the chicken pieces to the pan, cover and simmer for about 20 minutes, or until the rice is tender and has absorbed all the liquid and the chicken is cooked. Keep checking the pan and stirring the rice to prevent it from sticking, adding more stock or water if necessary. Serve hot, sprinkled with peanuts and chilli.

grilled chicken creole

1   To prepare the seasoning, put the spring onions, onion, garlic, chilli, herbs and allspice berries into a bowl. Add the lime juice and olive oil and stir well.

2   With a sharp knife, slash the chicken breasts 2–3 times on both sides, and season lightly with salt and pepper. Rub the seasoning over both sides of each breast, pressing it into the slashes. Cover and marinate in the refrigerator for 2–3 hours.

3   Put the chicken breasts on a grill pan and cook under a preheated hot grill, turning once, until cooked. Take care that the herbs do not burn. Alternatively, cook them in a preheated oven, 200°C (400°F), Gas Mark 6, for about 20 minutes.

4   While the chicken is cooking, make the avocado sauce. Peel, halve and pit the avocado. Mash the flesh to a smooth paste and beat in the onion, garlic and a little cayenne pepper. Add a little lime juice to prevent the sauce from discolouring. Serve the chicken with the sauce and with some rice.

6 boneless, skinless chicken breasts

salt and pepper

Creole Seasoning:

2 spring onions, finely chopped

½ red onion, finely chopped

2 garlic cloves, crushed

1 red chilli, deseeded and finely chopped

3 chives, snipped

few thyme sprigs, chopped

few parsley sprigs, chopped

3 allspice berries, crushed

juice of 1 lime

2 tablespoons olive oil

Avocado Sauce:

1 large ripe avocado

1 tablespoon finely chopped onion

½ garlic clove, crushed

cayenne pepper, to taste

lime juice

Serves 6

Preparation time: 20 minutes, plus marinating

Cooking time: 15–20 minutes

3 tablespoons vegetable oil

4 garlic cloves, crushed

3 shallots, chopped

3 lemon grass stalks, very finely chopped

6 kaffir lime leaves, shredded

3 tablespoons ready-made green curry paste

1 tablespoon Thai fish sauce

2 teaspoons palm sugar or soft brown sugar

250 ml (8 fl oz) chicken stock

8 large chicken drumsticks

To Garnish:

1 red chilli, sliced

kaffir lime leaves (optional)

lemon grass stalks

Serves 4
Preparation time: 15 minutes
Cooking time: about 1 hour

1 Heat the oil in a large flameproof casserole, add the garlic and shallots and fry over a gentle heat, stirring constantly, for 3 minutes, or until just softened.

2 Add the lemon grass, lime leaves, curry paste, fish sauce and sugar to the pan. Fry for 1 minute, then add the stock and chicken drumsticks and bring the curry to the boil. Reduce the heat, cover and simmer gently, stirring occasionally, for 40–45 minutes, until the chicken is tender and cooked through.

3 Season to taste with salt and pepper and serve the curry garnished with chilli slices, lime leaves, if using, and lemon grass stalks. Serve with noodles or rice.

phuket chicken curry

devilled chicken

1 To prepare the chicken, first remove the wings at the first joint, then lay the chicken upside down. Make a lengthways cut alongside the backbone and open up the chicken. Cut along the other side of the backbone to remove it completely. Remove the shoulder bones from each side. Finally, carefully remove the breastbone, taking care not to pierce through the chicken skin. Make 2 incisions along each leg, one along the thigh bone and one along the leg bone to ensure that both the breasts and legs will be cooked in the same time. Cut a hole in the skin between the point of the breast and the thigh and push the tip of the drumstick through to secure the leg. Trim any fat and neaten.

2 Combine the oil, mustards, Worcestershire sauce, vinegar, onion, honey, Tabasco sauce, garlic, and salt and pepper to taste. Brush both sides of the chicken with half the sauce and place in a roasting tin, skin side up. Cook in a preheated oven, 180°C (350°F), Gas Mark 4, for about 45 minutes, or until the thigh juices run clear when pierced.

3 Transfer the chicken, skin side up, to a grill pan and brush the skin with the remaining sauce. Grill for 2–3 minutes until crisp and brown.

4 To serve, cut in half and garnish with the watercress.

1.5 kg (3 lb) chicken

3 tablespoons cooking oil

1 tablespoon English mustard powder

1 tablespoon Dijon mustard

1 teaspoon Worcestershire sauce

1 teaspoon white wine vinegar

1 teaspoon grated onion

1 teaspoon clear honey

½–1 teaspoon Tabasco sauce

1 garlic clove, finely chopped

salt and pepper

1 bunch of watercress, to garnish

Serves 2

Preparation time: 15–20 minutes

Cooking time: about 50 minutes

spicy pot roast chicken

1 Heat the butter and oil in a flameproof casserole and fry the onions until brown. Add the garlic and ginger and fry for 1 minute. Then add the garam masala and coriander and fry for a further minute. Stir in the tomatoes and chillies. Season to taste with salt and pepper and fry for 2–3 minutes. Place the chicken in the pan and seal all over, basting thoroughly with the mixture.

2 Cover the casserole and transfer to a preheated oven, 180°C (350°F), Gas Mark 4, for about 1–1¼ hours, until the chicken is tender, basting once or twice. Remove the lid for the last 20 minutes to brown.

3 Garnish with coriander sprigs and serve the sauce separately.

50 g (2 oz) butter

50 ml (2 fl oz) oil

2 large onions, sliced

2 garlic cloves, crushed

50 g (2 oz) piece of fresh ginger, finely chopped

1 tablespoon garam masala

1 tablespoon ground coriander

8 tomatoes, skinned and chopped (see page 24)

2 green chillies, deseeded and chopped

1.75 kg (3½ lb) chicken

salt and pepper

coriander sprigs, to garnish

Serves 4
Preparation time: 15 minutes
Cooking time: 1½ hours

8 large chicken wings

salt and pepper

Marinade:

1 garlic clove

5 cm (2 inch) piece of fresh root ginger, roughly chopped

juice and finely grated rind of 1 lemon

2 tablespoons light soy sauce

2 tablespoons groundnut oil

2 teaspoons ground cinnamon

1 teaspoon ground turmeric

2 tablespoons clear honey

Yellow Pepper Dip:

2 yellow peppers

4 tablespoons natural yogurt

1 tablespoon dark soy sauce

1 tablespoon chopped coriander

Serves 2–4

Preparation time: 30 minutes, plus marinating

Cooking time: 8–10 minutes

---

1 Put all the marinade ingredients into a food processor or blender and purée until very smooth. Place the chicken in a bowl, pour over the marinade and toss well. Cover and leave to marinate for 1–2 hours.

2 To make the yellow pepper dip, put the yellow peppers under a preheated grill for about 10 minutes, turning until well charred and blistered. Put them into a plastic bag and leave until cool, then peel off the skins and discard the seeds. Put the flesh into a food processor or blender with the yogurt and purée until smooth. Pour into a bowl, season with the soy sauce and pepper to taste, then stir in the coriander. Set aside.

3 Drain the chicken and cook under a preheated hot grill for 4–5 minutes on each side, basting with the remaining marinade. Serve with the yellow pepper dip.

spiced chicken wings & pepper dip

red hot turkey sandwich

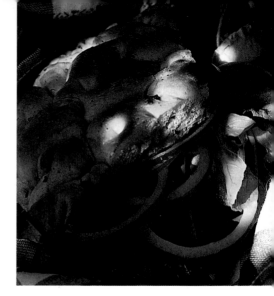

1 To make the mayonnaise, whisk the egg yolks and vinegar until slightly thickened. Continue to whisk, adding the sunflower oil in a thin steady stream until the mixture forms a thick creamy mayonnaise. Cover and set aside. Place the garlic, pine nuts and Parmesan in a food processor or blender and purée until smooth. Add the sun-dried tomato halves and chillies and purée until smooth. With the motor running, gradually add 3 tablespoons of the oil from the tomatoes. Spoon the mixture into a bowl and stir in the mayonnaise. Cover and set aside.

2 Place the turkey in a single layer in a shallow dish. Mix the olive oil and orange juice in a jug. Pour over the mixture and turn to coat. Cover and marinate for 30–60 minutes.

3 Drain the turkey, reserving the marinade, then cook the escalopes under a preheated hot grill for 3–4 minutes on each side, or until tender, basting frequently with the marinade. Remove from the heat, cut into thin strips and keep hot. Slice the bread in half and toast both halves on the crumb side. Spread each half with some mayonnaise. Divide the artichokes between the bread halves and add the red onion, rocket and sliced hot turkey. Sprinkle with salt and pepper to taste and serve.

4 x 125 g (4 oz) turkey escalopes

4 tablespoons olive oil

3 tablespoons orange juice

1 large loaf of focaccia or olive bread

4 artichoke hearts in oil, drained and sliced

1 red onion, thinly sliced into rings

125 g (4 oz) rocket

salt and pepper

Red Hot Mayonnaise:

2 egg yolks

1 tablespoon white wine vinegar

200 ml (7 fl oz) sunflower oil

2 garlic cloves, crushed

25 g (1 oz) pine nuts

4 tablespoons grated Parmesan cheese

8 sun-dried tomato halves in oil

2 red chillies, peeled (see page 28) and deseeded

Serves 4
Preparation time: 20 minutes, plus marinating
Cooking time: 6–8 minutes

- meat-stuffed tortillas
- chilli stir-fry with steak
- chilli con carne
- mexican beef with lime rice
- lamb casserole with roasted garlic & chilli
- chorizo kebabs with celeriac & garlic purée
- chilli pork
- griddled sausages & mustard mash
- sweet & spicy pork

meat with a kick

meat-stuffed tortillas

1 Put the minced pork and beef into a large frying pan and cook in their own fat until browned and crumbly, breaking up the meat with a wooden spoon. Add the oil, onion and garlic and cook until soft. Stir in the chilli powder, cumin, oregano and salt, then the vinegar and stock. Simmer for 10 minutes, or until the liquid has evaporated. Remove from the heat and leave to cool.

2 Spread some of the salsa cruda over each tortilla and put about 2 tablespoons of the meat filling down the centre of each one. Fold over, secure with a cocktail stick and arrange in an ovenproof dish.

3 Pour the remaining salsa cruda over the tortillas and sprinkle over the grated Cheddar. Bake in a preheated oven, 180°C (350°F), Gas Mark 4, for 20–30 minutes, until golden brown. Remove the tortillas from the dish and garnish with the radish or olive slices, chilli flakes and red chilli slices.

500 g (1 lb) minced pork

500 g (1 lb) minced beef

1 tablespoon olive oil

1 large onion, finely chopped

2 garlic cloves, crushed

1 tablespoon chilli powder

½ teaspoon ground cumin

2 teaspoons dried oregano

pinch of salt

50 ml (2 fl oz) vinegar

250 ml (8 fl oz) beef stock

450 ml (¾ pint) Salsa Cruda (see page 9)

12 ready-made corn or wheat tortillas

75 g (3 oz) Cheddar cheese, grated

To Garnish:

sliced radishes or olives

dried chilli flakes

1 red chilli, deseeded and finely sliced

Serves 4
Preparation time: 20 minutes
Cooking time: 30–40 minutes

chilli stir-fry with steak

1 Heat the oil in a wok. Add the diced steak, a little at a time, and stir-fry until sealed all over. Add the garlic and stir-fry for about 2 minutes, until it has blended with the meat; add the ginger and stir-fry for 2 minutes more. Sprinkle in all the spices, and stir-fry until the pieces of meat are coated in them. The meat should be dry without sticking to the pan. Strain the tomatoes and use the juice to moisten the meat if necessary.

2 Add the onion, a tablespoon at a time, allowing each spoonful to be absorbed by the meat before adding the next. Stir-fry for another 3–4 minutes. By now the meat should have cooked for about 20 minutes and will be half cooked. Add the remaining tomato juice, the tomatoes, chillies and chilli powder to taste. Season with salt to taste, cover and continue to cook for about 20 minutes, or until the meat is tender. Serve immediately.

4 tablespoons vegetable oil

750 g (1½ lb) lean sirloin steak, diced

2–3 garlic cloves, finely chopped

5 cm (2 inch) piece of fresh root ginger, finely chopped

2 teaspoons coriander seeds, toasted and ground

1 teaspoon cumin seeds, toasted and ground

½ teaspoon fennel seeds, toasted and ground

½ teaspoon fenugreek, toasted and ground

1 teaspoon ground turmeric

2 teaspoons paprika

400 g (13 oz) can tomatoes

1 large onion, very finely chopped

2–6 fresh green chillies, chopped

2–4 teaspoons chilli powder

salt

Serves 4

Preparation time: 30 minutes

Cooking time: about 40 minutes

chilli con carne

1 Heat the oil in a saucepan, add the onions, red pepper and garlic and fry gently until soft. Add the meat and fry until just coloured.

2 Blend in the stock and add the chilli powder, beans, tomatoes, cumin and salt and pepper to taste. Bring to the boil, cover, lower the heat and simmer gently for 50–60 minutes, stirring occasionally.

3 Meanwhile, boil the rice for 10 minutes, or according to the packet instructions, in plenty of lightly salted boiling water until tender. Drain well. Serve the chilli con carne on a bed of rice, with the soured cream, chilli seeds and grated Cheddar. Garnish with the spring onion.

■ Since the seeds are the hottest part of a chilli, only use them as a garnish if you and your guests have a taste for quite fiery food.

2 tablespoons oil

3 onions, chopped

1 red pepper, cored, deseeded and diced

2 garlic cloves, crushed

500 g (1 lb) lean minced beef

450 ml (¾ pint) beef stock

1 teaspoon chilli powder

475 g (15 oz) cooked red kidney beans

400 g (13 oz) can chopped tomatoes

½ teaspoon ground cumin

250 g (8 oz) long-grain rice

salt and pepper

finely chopped spring onion, to garnish

To Serve:

soured cream

chilli seeds (optional)

grated Cheddar cheese

Serves 4
Preparation time: 15 minutes
Cooking time: 1¼ hours

2 tablespoons vegetable oil

500 g (1 lb) lean minced beef

1 onion, finely chopped

1 red or green pepper, cored, deseeded and diced

2 garlic cloves, finely chopped

1 tablespoon tomato purée

½ teaspoon chilli powder, or to taste

1 teaspoon cumin seeds, toasted

150 g (5 oz) frozen sweetcorn kernels

250 g (8 oz) cooked or canned red kidney beans

475 ml (16 fl oz) vegetable stock

250 g (8 oz) long-grain rice

300 ml (½ pint) water

juice of 2 limes

3 tablespoons finely chopped coriander leaves

salt and pepper

½ green chilli, deseeded and finely sliced, to garnish

1 Heat the oil in a heavy-based saucepan, add the beef and fry, stirring frequently, until browned. Stir in the onion, red or green pepper and garlic, and fry until just soft. Add the tomato purée, chilli powder, cumin, sweetcorn, beans and vegetable stock and season to taste with salt and pepper. Bring to the boil, then simmer for 45 minutes, stirring occasionally.

2 When the beef has simmered for about 25 minutes, put the rice, water, lime juice and ½ teaspoon of salt into another saucepan. Bring to the boil and stir once. Cover and simmer for 15 minutes, or according to the packet instructions.

3 Lightly fluff up the rice with a fork and stir in the chopped coriander. Serve the beef garnished with the chilli strips and accompanied by a portion of lime rice.

Serves 4

Preparation time: 10 minutes

Cooking time: 1 hour

mexican beef with lime rice

lamb casserole with roasted garlic & chilli

1 Put the chillies and garlic on a baking sheet and roast in a preheated oven, 220°C (425°F), Gas Mark 7, for 15–20 minutes. Cool slightly then peel off the skins, and remove the seeds from the chillies. Put the chilli and garlic flesh into a small bowl with the coriander and cumin seeds and mash to a paste.

2 Heat 1 tablespoon of the oil in a heavy-based saucepan, add the lamb cubes and brown. Remove the lamb and set aside. Heat the remaining oil in the pan and gently fry the onion for 5 minutes. Add the chilli paste and stir-fry for another minute.

3 Return the lamb to the pan and add the rice, chickpeas, tomatoes, aubergine, beans, stock and season to taste. Bring to the boil, then cover and simmer gently for 1–1½ hours, or until tender. Stir in the coriander. Serve with the yogurt and garnish each serving with a red chilli.

2 large red or green chillies

2 large garlic cloves, unpeeled

1 teaspoon coriander seeds, toasted and crushed

1 teaspoon cumin seeds, toasted and crushed

3 tablespoons vegetable oil

750 g (1½ lb) boneless lamb, cubed

1 onion, chopped

375 g (12 oz) cooked brown long-grain rice

125 g (4 oz) cooked chickpeas

400 g (13 oz) can chopped tomatoes

1 large aubergine, diced

75 g (3 oz) green beans, chopped

450 ml (¾ pint) vegetable stock

3 tablespoons finely chopped coriander leaves

salt and pepper

red chillies, to garnish

natural yogurt, to serve

Serves 4
Preparation time: 20 minutes
Cooking time: about 1½–2 hours

1   Place the celeriac in a saucepan. Cover with lightly salted cold water and bring to the boil. Cover the pan, lower the heat and simmer for 15–20 minutes, until tender. Drain and add the garlic. Add the butter, season to taste with salt and pepper and mash well. Transfer the purée to a warmed bowl.

2   Heat a griddle pan. Cut each onion into 8 wedges, cutting almost, but not all the way through, so they remain attached at the root end. Place the onion wedges on the griddle and cook for about 4 minutes on each side, or until they are charred. If they are charring too much, reduce the heat.

3   Meanwhile, thread the lengths of sausage on to 4 long metal skewers, alternating with sage leaves. Cook under a preheated hot grill for 8–10 minutes, turning occasionally, until slightly crisp and heated through.

4   Serve the griddled onions and sausage kebabs with the celeriac purée.

750 g (1½ lb) celeriac, peeled and cut into 2.5 cm (1 inch) cubes

8 large garlic cloves, roasted (see page 62)

25 g (1 oz) butter

4 red onions, unpeeled

4 large chorizo or merguez sausages, cut into 2.5 cm (1 inch) lengths

1 bunch of sage, leaves stripped from the stalks

salt and pepper

Serves 4

Preparation time: 30 minutes

Cooking time: 20 minutes

chorizo kebabs with celeriac & garlic purée

3 tablespoons vegetable oil

125 g (4 oz) minced pork

2 tomatoes, diced

5 teaspoons sugar

5 teaspoons Thai fish sauce

coriander leaves, to garnish

Chilli Paste:

5 small shallots

15 g (½ oz) large dried red chillies, soaked for 20 minutes

12 coriander roots

Salad:

½ cucumber, cut into chunks

1 little gem lettuce, separated into leaves

coriander sprigs

1 To make the chilli paste, put the shallots, chillies and coriander roots into a food processor or blender and purée, adding a little water if the mixture seems very dry. Alternatively, pound them together in a mortar until thoroughly amalgamated.

2 Heat the oil in a wok, add the chilli paste and stir-fry for 30 seconds. Add the pork and tomatoes and cook, stirring, for 30 seconds, then add the sugar and fish sauce and continue to cook, stirring, for 4–5 minutes.

3 Turn the pork into a bowl, garnish with coriander and serve, with the salad arranged on a separate plate.

Serves 2
Preparation time: 10 minutes
Cooking time: 6–8 minutes

chilli pork

■ This recipe could be served as part of a Thai meal. Serve it with a noodle dish, such as Prawns & Noodles in Spicy Broth (see page 29) or Chiang Mai Noodles (see page 78).

griddled sausages & mustard mash

1 Heat a griddle pan. Put the potatoes into a saucepan of cold water, bring to the boil and simmer for 15 minutes.

2 Meanwhile, place the sausages on the griddle and cook for 10 minutes, turning occasionally. Add the onion wedges and cook with the sausages for 6–7 minutes.

3 When the potatoes are cooked, drain them well and return to the pan. Put the pan over a low heat so that any excess water steams away, without colouring the potatoes. Remove from the heat; peel the potatoes and mash well. Add the butter, mustards and garlic and season with salt and pepper and continue to mash. Taste the potato and add more mustard if liked, then add the parsley and a dash of olive oil and stir. Serve the mash and sausages with the griddled onion wedges.

■ It is well worth investing in a ridged cast-iron griddle pan. Not only is griddling a quick and easy way of cooking, but it is also a healthy one, and the results look good as well.

8 speciality sausages

2 onions, cut into wedges, roots left intact

Mustard Mash:

1 kg (2 lb) potatoes, quartered but unpeeled

75 g (3 oz) butter

1 tablespoon wholegrain mustard

1 tablespoon prepared English mustard

1 garlic clove, crushed

1 large bunch of parsley, chopped

dash of olive oil

sea salt and pepper

Serves 4
Preparation time: 10 minutes
Cooking time: 25 minutes

sweet & spicy pork

1 Cut the pork fillet crossways into 2 cm (¾ inch) slices, then cut these slices crossways into 2–3 strips. Mix the sauce ingredients in a measuring jug, add cold water up to the 250 ml (8 fl oz) mark and mix well.

2 Heat a wok until hot. Add the oil and heat until very hot. Add the spring onions, ginger and garlic and stir-fry over a moderate heat for about 1 minute. Add the carrots and stir-fry for 1–2 minutes.

3 Increase the heat to high, add the pork and stir-fry for about 5 minutes. Pour in the sauce mixture and bring to the boil, stirring all the time, then simmer for about 2 minutes, or until the sauce is thick and reduced. Taste, and add more chilli sauce, if liked.

4 Add the bean sprouts and toss vigorously to mix all the ingredients together. Sprinkle with the pomegranate seeds, if using, and serve immediately.

1 pork fillet (tenderloin), weighing about 375 g (12 oz)

4 tablespoons groundnut oil

5 spring onions, chopped

2.5 cm (1 inch) piece of fresh root ginger, finely chopped

2 garlic cloves, finely chopped

3 carrots, thinly sliced

125 g (4 oz) bean sprouts

seeds of 1 pomegranate (optional)

Chilli-Soy Sauce:

4 tablespoons rice wine or sherry

2–3 tablespoons soy sauce

2–3 tablespoons chilli sauce

2 tablespoons clear honey

1 tablespoon tomato purée

2 teaspoons cornflour

Serves 4

Preparation time: 30 minutes

Cooking time: about 15 minutes

black bean chilli ●

spiced coleslaw ●

spicy potatoes ●

vegetable fajitas ●

balti mixed vegetables ●

balti courgettes ●

kidney bean curry ●

chiang mai noodles ●

vegetable biryani ●

vegetable curry ●

sizzling vegetables

black bean chilli

1 Put the beans into a pan with the water and bring to the boil. Boil rapidly for 10 minutes, then reduce the heat, cover the pan and simmer for 45 minutes.

2 Meanwhile, heat half the oil in a saucepan and stir-fry the mushrooms for 5 minutes. Remove from the pan and reserve. Add the remaining oil to the pan with the onion, garlic, potatoes, red or green pepper and spices and fry over a moderate heat for 10 minutes.

3 Drain the beans, reserving the liquid. Boil the liquid until reduced to 450 ml (¾ pint). Stir the beans into the pan with the vegetables and add the reduced cooking liquid, passata and mushrooms. Bring to the boil, cover and simmer for 30 minutes.

4 Stir in the lime juice, chocolate and coriander and cook for a further 5 minutes. Serve hot topped with a spoon of avocado salsa, if using.

250 g (8 oz) dried black beans, soaked overnight and drained

1.5 litres (2½ pints) water

4 tablespoons extra virgin olive oil

250 g (8 oz) small mushrooms, halved

1 large onion, chopped

2 garlic cloves, crushed

2 large potatoes, cubed

1 red or green pepper, cored, deseeded and diced

2 teaspoons ground coriander

1 teaspoon ground cumin

2 teaspoons hot chilli powder

450 ml (¾ pint) passata (sieved tomatoes)

1 tablespoon lime juice

25 g (1 oz) dark chocolate, chopped

2 tablespoons finely chopped coriander leaves

Avocado Salsa (see page 15), to serve (optional)

Serves 8

Preparation time: 20 minutes, plus soaking and making the salsa (optional)

Cooking time: 1½ hours

■ Chocolate is a traditional ingredient used in some savoury Mexican and Spanish dishes. Use a bitter, unsweetened chocolate.

Dressing:

3 tablespoons mayonnaise

½ teaspoon curry powder

½ teaspoon ground nutmeg

½ teaspoon paprika

1 teaspoon English mustard powder

1 tablespoon olive oil

1 tablespoon lemon juice

salt and pepper

Salad:

¼–½ white cabbage or cabbage heart

1 unpeeled dessert apple, cored and diced

2 carrots, grated

2 tablespoons diced gherkins

2 teaspoons capers

2 tablespoons chopped parsley

Serves 4
Preparation time: 25–30 minutes

1 First make the dressing. Mix together all of the ingredients in a measuring jug.

2 Shred the cabbage finely by hand, or use a food processor or blender, then put it into a serving bowl. Add the apple and carrots with the gherkins, capers and parsley. Pour the dressing over and mix thoroughly. Serve immediately.

spiced coleslaw

■ Don't make the coleslaw too far in advance, as the cabbage and other salad ingredients should be served as fresh and crisp as possible.

spicy potatoes

1 Heat the oil in a heavy-based saucepan, add the mustard seeds and fry until they pop; this should only take a few seconds. Add the potatoes and fry for about 5 minutes. Add the spices, lemon juice, sugar and salt to taste, stir well and cook for 5 minutes.

2 Add the tomatoes, stir well, then simmer for 5–10 minutes, until the potatoes are tender. Serve garnished with coriander leaves.

■ Turmeric is often regarded as a poor man's saffron – largely because it is so much less expensive. It has a more bitter taste than saffron and is an ingredient in commercial curry powders. Be careful not to spill it as it will stain clothes and work surfaces.

2 tablespoons vegetable oil

½ teaspoon mustard seeds

250 g (8 oz) potatoes, cut into small cubes

1 teaspoon ground turmeric

1 teaspoon chilli powder

2 teaspoons paprika

4 tablespoons lemon juice

1 teaspoon sugar

250 g (8 oz) tomatoes, quartered

salt

2 tablespoons chopped coriander leaves, to garnish

Serves 4
Preparation time: 10 minutes
Cooking time: 20 minutes

vegetable fajitas

1 Heat the olive oil in a large frying pan and gently sauté the onions and garlic for about 5 minutes, until soft and golden brown.

2 Add the red and green peppers, chillies and oregano or coriander and stir well. Sauté gently for about 10 minutes, until cooked and just tender.

3 Add the mushrooms and cook quickly for 1 minute more, stirring to mix the mushrooms thoroughly with the other vegetables. Season the vegetable mixture with salt and pepper to taste.

4 To serve, spoon the sizzling hot vegetable mixture into the warmed tortillas and roll up or fold over. Serve hot, garnished with chives.

2 tablespoons olive oil

2 large onions, thinly sliced

2 garlic cloves, crushed

2 red peppers, cored, deseeded and thinly sliced

2 green peppers, cored, deseeded and thinly sliced

4 green chillies, deseeded and thinly sliced

2 teaspoons chopped oregano or coriander

250 g (8 oz) button mushrooms, sliced

salt and pepper

12 warmed ready-made tortillas, to serve

chives, to garnish

Serves 4

Preparation time: 15 minutes

Cooking time: 15–20 minutes

1 Heat the oil in a wok or heavy-based saucepan and gently fry the onion for 5–10 minutes, or until lightly browned.

2 Add the garlic, ginger, chilli powder, coriander, turmeric and a pinch of salt. Fry for 2–3 minutes, then add the diced vegetables and stir-fry for a further 2–3 minutes.

3 Add the chopped tomatoes, stir well and add a little water. Cover and cook gently for 10–12 minutes, or until the vegetables are tender, adding a little more water, if necessary, to prevent the vegetables from sticking to the base of the wok. Serve immediately with Indian bread.

2–3 tablespoons vegetable oil

1 small onion, chopped

1 garlic clove, crushed

2.5 cm (1 inch) piece of fresh root ginger, grated

1 teaspoon chilli powder

2 teaspoons ground coriander

½ teaspoon ground turmeric

500 g (1 lb) diced mixed vegetables (e.g. potatoes, carrots, swede, peas, beans, cauliflower)

2–3 tomatoes, skinned and chopped (see page 24)

salt

Indian bread, to serve

Serves 4

Preparation time: 15 minutes

Cooking time: 20–30 minutes

balti mixed vegetables

balti courgettes

1 Heat the ghee or butter in a balti pan or heavy-based frying pan, add the onion and fry for 5 minutes, stirring occasionally, until softened.

2 Add the asafoetida, if using, then add the potatoes and fry for 2–3 minutes.

3 Stir in the sliced courgettes, the chilli powder, turmeric, coriander and salt. Add the water, cover the pan and cook gently for 8–10 minutes, until the potatoes are tender. Sprinkle with the garam masala and garnish with chopped coriander. Serve immediately with Indian bread.

25 g (1 oz) ghee or butter

1 small onion, chopped

pinch of asafoetida (optional)

2 small potatoes, quartered

375 g (12 oz) courgettes, sliced

½ teaspoon chilli powder

½ teaspoon ground turmeric

1 teaspoon ground coriander

½ teaspoon salt

150 ml (¼ pint) water

½ teaspoon garam masala

chopped coriander leaves, to garnish

Indian bread, to serve

Serves 4

Preparation time: 10 minutes

Cooking time: about 15 minutes

125 ml (4 fl oz) vegetable oil

2 teaspoons cumin seeds

1 large onion, chopped

400 g (13 oz) can chopped tomatoes

1 tablespoon ground coriander

1 teaspoon chilli powder

1 teaspoon sugar

1 teaspoon salt

2 x 425 g (14 oz) cans red kidney beans, drained and rinsed

coriander, to garnish

To Serve:

boiled rice

soured cream

Serves 4–6
Preparation time: 15 minutes
Cooking time: 30–35 minutes

1 Heat the oil in a wok or frying pan, add the cumin seeds and chopped onion and fry until the onion is lightly browned. Stir in the tomatoes and fry for a few seconds, then add the ground coriander, chilli powder, sugar and salt and stir well. Lower the heat and cook for about 5–7 minutes.

2 Add the drained kidney beans, stir carefully but thoroughly and cook for 10–15 minutes. Garnish with coriander and serve with rice and a dollop of soured cream.

kidney bean curry

chiang mai noodles

1 Cook the noodles in boiling water for 5–6 minutes. Drain and rinse in cold water to stop further cooking and drain again.

2 Heat the oil in a wok, add the garlic and stir-fry until golden. Add the curry paste and chillies and mix thoroughly. Pour in the coconut milk, stirring continuously, then bring to the boil and cook until the liquid thickens a little.

3 Add the stock, turmeric, curry powder, fish or soy sauce and sugar and bring back to the boil. Lower the heat and add the celery, shallot, red pepper, mushrooms and peanuts. Bring back to the boil, then remove from the heat.

4 To serve, put the noodles into a large serving bowl, pour the sauce over them and sprinkle with lime juice to taste.

■ To prepare the nuts, dry-fry unroasted peanuts in a preheated wok, stirring, until they turn golden. Remove from the heat. When cooled, put them in a polythene bag and crush with a rolling pin. Store for up to 1 month in an airtight container in the refrigerator.

175 g (6 oz) dried egg noodles

1 tablespoon groundnut oil

2 garlic cloves, finely chopped

2 tablespoons Red Curry Paste (see page 8)

¼ teaspoon crushed dried chillies

250 ml (8 fl oz) coconut milk

500 ml (17 fl oz) vegetable stock

¼ teaspoon ground turmeric

1½ teaspoons curry powder

2 tablespoons Thai fish sauce or soy sauce

15 g (½ oz) palm sugar or light muscovado sugar

25 g (1 oz) celery stick, chopped

25 g (1 oz) shallot, finely sliced

25 g (1 oz) red pepper, chopped

25 g (1 oz) dried shiitake mushrooms, soaked, drained and sliced

1 tablespoon crushed roasted peanuts (see below)

2 tablespoons lime juice, to serve

Serves 4 as part of a Thai meal

Preparation time: 30 minutes, plus soaking

Cooking time: 15 minutes

vegetable biryani

1 Bring a large saucepan of salted water to a rolling boil, add the basmati rice and return to a simmer. Cook gently for 5 minutes. Drain, refresh under cold water and drain again. Spread the rice on a large baking sheet and set aside to dry.

2 Heat 2 tablespoons of the oil in a frying pan, add half the onion and fry over a moderate heat for 10 minutes, until very crisp and golden. Remove and drain on kitchen paper. Reserve for garnishing.

3 Add the rest of the oil to the pan and fry the remaining onion with the garlic and ginger for 5 minutes. Add the sweet potato, carrots and spices and fry for a further 10 minutes, until light golden. Add the stock and tomatoes and bring to the boil. Cover the pan and simmer gently for 20 minutes. Add the cauliflower and peas and cook for 8–10 minutes, until all the vegetables are tender.

4 Stir in the rice, cashew nuts and coriander. Cook, stirring, for 3 minutes, then cover and remove from the heat. Leave to stand for 5 minutes, then serve garnished with the crispy onions and egg quarters.

250 g (8 oz) basmati rice, rinsed

6 tablespoons sunflower oil

2 large onions, thinly sliced

2 garlic cloves, crushed

2 teaspoons grated fresh root ginger

250 g (8 oz) sweet potato, diced

2 large carrots, diced

1 tablespoon curry paste

2 teaspoons ground turmeric

1 teaspoon ground cinnamon

1 teaspoon chilli powder

300 ml (½ pint) vegetable stock

4 ripe tomatoes, skinned, deseeded and diced (see page 24)

175 g (6 oz) cauliflower florets

125 g (4 oz) frozen peas, thawed

50 g (2 oz) cashew nuts, toasted

2 tablespoons chopped coriander

salt

2 hard-boiled eggs, quartered, to serve

Serves 4
Preparation time: 25 minutes
Cooking time: about 1 hour

1 Heat the oil for deep-frying to 180–190°C (350–375°F), or until a cube of bread browns in 30 seconds. Deep-fry the tofu cubes in batches for about 1 minute, until they are crisp and golden. Remove with a slotted spoon, drain thoroughly on kitchen paper and set aside.

2 Heat the vegetable oil in a heavy-based saucepan, add the shallots, chillies, garlic, ginger and lemon grass and fry over a gentle heat, stirring frequently, for 5 minutes, until just softened.

3 Add the ground spices, chilli powder and shrimp paste and fry for 1 further minute. Stir in the stock and coconut milk and bring to the boil. Add the potatoes, reduce the heat and cook for 6 minutes. Add the beans and cook for 8 minutes.

4 Stir in the cabbage, bean sprouts, rice vermicelli and season with salt to taste. Cook gently for 3 minutes. Stir in the fried tofu and serve immediately.

oil, for deep-frying

4 squares of yellow tofu cut into 2.5 cm (1 inch) cubes

2 tablespoons vegetable oil

4 shallots, sliced

2 green chillies, deseeded and sliced

3 garlic cloves, chopped

1 tablespoon finely chopped fresh root ginger

1 lemon grass stalk, finely chopped

1 tablespoon ground coriander

1 teaspoon ground cumin

1 teaspoon ground turmeric

1 teaspoon galangal (laos) powder

1 teaspoon chilli powder

1 teaspoon shrimp paste

600 ml (1 pint) vegetable stock

400 ml (14 fl oz) coconut milk

250 g (8 oz) potatoes, diced

125 g (4 oz) green beans, cut into 1 cm (½ inch) lengths

125 g (4 oz) white cabbage, finely shredded

75 g (3 oz) bean sprouts

25 g (1 oz) dried rice vermicelli, soaked in boiling water for 5 minutes, then drained

salt

Serves 6

Preparation time: 20 minutes

Cooking time: 35 minutes

vegetable curry

tagliatelle with chilli balsamic sauce ●

pasta with calabrian sauce ●

fettuccine with spicy tomato sauce ●

peppery chicken with pasta ●

chinese beef cappellini ●

indian meatballs with tomato curry sauce ●

penne all'arrabbiata ●

quick focaccia pizza with pepperoni ●

chilli-topped pizza ●

spicy hot pizza ●

pasta
& pizza

375 g (12 oz) dried tagliatelle

4 tablespoons olive oil

2 garlic cloves, crushed

2 red chillies, deseeded
and chopped

4 tablespoons balsamic vinegar

2 tablespoons orange juice

3 tablespoons ready-made red pesto

1 bunch of spring onions, shredded

25 g (1 oz) toasted hazelnuts,
chopped

salt

grated Parmesan cheese,
to serve (optional)

1 Cook the pasta in plenty of lightly salted boiling water for 8–12 minutes, or according to the packet instructions, until just tender.

2 Meanwhile, heat the oil in a saucepan. Add the garlic and chillies and fry for 2 minutes. Reduce the heat and stir in the vinegar, orange juice, red pesto, shredded spring onions and chopped hazelnuts. Season to taste with salt.

3 Drain the tagliatelle and pile into a warmed bowl. Pour over the sauce and toss well. Sprinkle with grated Parmesan, if liked.

Serves 4
Preparation time: 10 minutes
Cooking time: 8–12 minutes

tagliatelle with chilli balsamic sauce

pasta with calabrian sauce

1 Crush the tomatoes or purée them briefly in a food processor or blender. Coat the base of a saucepan with olive oil. Add the garlic and chilli and fry gently until the garlic is golden, crushing the chilli against the base of the pan to release its flavour. Add the tomatoes and the slices of salami and season to taste with salt. Simmer gently for about 30 minutes, until the sauce thickens and darkens in colour.

2 Meanwhile, cook the pasta in lightly salted boiling water for 8–12 minutes, or according to the packet instructions, until just tender.

3 Drain the pasta, transfer to a warmed serving dish and pour the sauce over the top. Serve with pecorino shavings and a generous grinding of pepper.

625 g (1¼ lb) canned tomatoes

olive oil, for frying

2 garlic cloves, each cut into 3–4 pieces

1 chilli, deseeded

125 g (4 oz) salami, thickly sliced

500 g (1 lb) dried conchiglie or other pasta shapes

salt and pepper

pecorino cheese shavings, to serve

Serves 4–6

Preparation time: 15 minutes

Cooking time: about 35 minutes

1 Cook the pasta in plenty of lightly salted boiling water for 8–12 minutes, or according to the packet instructions, until just tender.

2 Meanwhile, heat the oil in a large frying pan. Add the garlic, chilli powder and coriander. Fry over a moderate heat for 1 minute, stirring constantly. Stir in the pepperoni, the tomatoes with their juices, passata and red wine, and season to taste with salt and pepper. Simmer, uncovered, for about 10 minutes.

3 Drain the pasta and add it to the sauce. Toss and season with more pepper, if liked. Add the basil and toss again to mix. Sprinkle with thyme to garnish. Serve immediately.

375 g (12 oz) dried fettuccine

2 tablespoons olive oil

3 garlic cloves, crushed

1 teaspoon mild chilli powder

1 teaspoon ground coriander

125 g (4 oz) sliced pepperoni

400 g (13 oz) can chopped tomatoes

6 tablespoons passata (sieved tomatoes)

4 tablespoons red wine

1 tablespoon basil leaves

salt and pepper

thyme sprigs, to garnish

Serves 4

Preparation time: 10 minutes

Cooking time: 12 minutes

fettuccine with spicy tomato sauce

peppery chicken with pasta

1 In a bowl, mix together the chilli powder, cayenne, turmeric and 1 teaspoon of the olive oil. Stir to form a paste. Add the chicken pieces and coat thoroughly in the spice mixture. Cover and set aside for 15 minutes.

2 Meanwhile, heat the remaining olive oil in a large frying pan. Add the onion and fry for 3 minutes, until softened but not coloured. Add the tomatoes with the can juices and the sugar. Strip the basil leaves from the stems. Set some leaves aside for the garnish. Chop the rest finely and add them to the pan. Boil the mixture rapidly for 5 minutes, stirring occasionally to break up the tomatoes.

3 Cook the pasta in plenty of lightly salted water boiling for 8–12 minutes, or according to the packet instructions, until just tender.

4 While the pasta is cooking, dry-fry the spicy chicken pieces in a nonstick frying pan for 10 minutes, or until crisp. Add to the sauce. Drain the pasta, drizzle with a little more oil and season to taste with salt and pepper. Arrange the pasta on a large, warmed serving platter and pour over the sauce. Serve immediately, garnished with the reserved basil leaves.

■ 'Pipe rigate' are small curved elbow-shaped pasta shapes with a ribbed or 'rigate' surface.

1 teaspoon chilli powder

1 teaspoon cayenne pepper

1 teaspoon ground turmeric

1 tablespoon olive oil, plus a little extra for drizzling

250 g (8 oz) skinless chicken breast, cut into bite-sized pieces

1 onion, chopped

400 g (13 oz) can plum tomatoes

1 teaspoon caster sugar

1 bunch of basil

375 g (12 oz) dried pipe rigate or other pasta shapes

salt and pepper

Serves 4
Preparation time: 15 minutes, plus marinating
Cooking time: 25–30 minutes

1   Cut the steaks into 5 mm (¼ inch) wide strips. In a bowl, mix together the red peppercorns, chilli powder, Szechuan powder, light soy sauce and sherry. Add the strips of steak to the marinade and toss to coat thoroughly.

2   Cook the pasta in plenty of lightly salted boiling water for 8–12 minutes, or according to the packet instructions, until just tender.

3   While the pasta is cooking, heat a wok. Add the oil and heat until a blue haze can be seen. Set aside a few of the shredded spring onions for the garnish and add the rest to the wok with the sliced peppers and stir-fry for 2 minutes. Then add the marinated beef and the marinade and stir-fry for 5 minutes.

4   Drain the pasta. Place in a large warmed serving bowl and spoon the beef and pepper mixture over the top. Garnish with the reserved shredded spring onions and serve immediately.

4 sirloin steaks, about 125 g (4 oz) each

1 tablespoon crushed red peppercorns

1 tablespoon mild chilli powder

1–2 tablespoons Szechuan powder

3 tablespoons light soy sauce

3 tablespoons dry sherry

375 g (12 oz) dried cappellini

2 teaspoons sesame or light vegetable oil

1 bunch of spring onions, shredded

1 red pepper, cored, deseeded and thinly sliced

1 green pepper, cored, deseeded and thinly sliced

salt

Serves 4

Preparation time: 10 minutes

Cooking time: 15–20 minutes

chinese beef cappellini

1 onion, grated

50 g (2 oz) Parmesan cheese, grated

500 g (1 lb) minced lean lamb

1 tablespoon tomato purée

1 teaspoon chilli sauce

1 tablespoon ground coriander

1 tablespoon ground cumin

4 tablespoons olive oil, plus extra for drizzling

375 g (12 oz) dried spaghetti

salt and pepper

Tomato Curry Sauce:

1 tablespoon olive oil

1 onion, finely chopped

2 garlic cloves, crushed

1 tablespoon curry powder

2 tablespoons tomato purée

400 g (13 oz) can chopped tomatoes

2 teaspoons garam masala

2 tablespoons finely chopped coriander leaves

coriander leaves, to garnish

Serves 4

Preparation time: 20 minutes

Cooking time: about 30 minutes

1 To make the meatballs, combine the onion, cheese, lamb, tomato purée, chilli sauce, ground coriander and cumin. Add salt and pepper, and mix thoroughly. With dampened hands, divide the mixture into 28–32 pieces and shape into small balls. Heat the oil in a large frying pan and fry the meatballs in 2 batches for 10 minutes each. Using a slotted spoon, transfer the meatballs to an ovenproof dish. Keep hot.

2 Bring at least 1.8 litres (3 pints) of water to the boil in a large saucepan. Add a dash of oil and a generous pinch of salt. Cook the pasta for 8–12 minutes, or according to the packet instructions, until just tender.

3 Meanwhile, make the sauce. Heat the oil in a frying pan, add the onion and garlic and fry for 3–5 minutes, until the onion has softened. Stir in the curry powder, tomato purée and chopped tomatoes. Simmer the sauce, uncovered, for 5–10 minutes, then sprinkle in the garam masala, followed by the chopped coriander. Stir well.

4 Drain the pasta, pile it in a heated bowl and drizzle with a little oil. Season to taste with pepper. Pour over the sauce and toss lightly. Serve with the meatballs and garnish with coriander leaves.

indian meatballs with tomato curry sauce

■ Minced lamb is available from most butchers and supermarkets, but often incorporates quite a lot of fat. For best results, buy a single piece of lean lamb and mince it yourself using a meat mincer or food processor.

1 Purée the tomatoes in a food processor or blender, then set aside until required.

2 In a large saucepan, melt the butter over a moderate heat. Add the onion and bacon and cook, stirring, for 5 minutes. Add the garlic and chilli, then cook, stirring occasionally, for a further 5 minutes, or until the onion is tender. Add the tomatoes, oregano and thyme and season to taste with salt and pepper. Cover and simmer for 30 minutes.

3 Meanwhile, cook the pasta in plenty of lightly salted boiling water for 8–12 minutes, or according to the packet instructions, until just tender. Drain well.

4 Add the pasta to the sauce and toss gently. Transfer to a warmed serving dish and sprinkle with the Parmesan. Garnish with the parsley and serve immediately.

2 x 400 g (13 oz) cans tomatoes, drained

25 g (1 oz) butter

1 onion, finely chopped

125 g (4 oz) streaky bacon, derinded and diced

2 garlic cloves, finely chopped

1–2 red chillies, finely chopped

1 tablespoon chopped oregano

1 tablespoon chopped thyme

375 g (12 oz) dried penne

125 g (4 oz) Parmesan cheese, grated

1 tablespoon chopped parsley, to garnish

salt and pepper

Serves 4
Preparation time: 10–15 minutes
Cooking time: 40 minutes

penne all'arrabbiata

■ Penne are hollow, quill-shaped pasta, available in a variety of sizes. The recipe title translation is 'angry pasta quills.'

quick focaccia pizza with pepperoni

1 In a bowl, combine the red peppers, sun-dried tomatoes, half of the Parmesan, the coriander or parsley, garlic and salt and pepper.

2 Put the slices of bread on to greased baking sheets and spread a little of the red pepper mixture over each one. Top with a few slices of pepperoni. Sprinkle with the remaining grated Parmesan and a little olive oil.

3 Bake in a preheated oven, 240°C (475°F), Gas Mark 9, for about 5–10 minutes, until bubbling. Serve hot or warm with a green salad.

■ If you cannot find bottled red peppers, you can use fresh ones but first roast them in a preheated oven, 180°C (350°F), Gas Mark 4, for 20 minutes, then remove the skins and seeds.

3 bottled red peppers, drained and sliced

3 sun-dried tomatoes in oil, diced

75 g (3 oz) Parmesan cheese, grated

3 tablespoons finely chopped coriander or flat leaf parsley

2 garlic cloves, finely chopped

12 slices focaccia or ciabatta bread

75 g (3 oz) pepperoni, thinly sliced

olive oil, for sprinkling

salt and pepper

green salad, to serve

Makes 12 focaccia pizzas

Preparation time: 10 minutes

Cooking time: 5–10 minutes

chilli-topped pizza

1 Heat the oil in a saucepan. Add the shallots and cook for 2 minutes. Stir in the chilli powder and minced beef and cook until browned, stirring occasionally. Add the tomatoes with their juice and the Tabasco sauce. Bring to the boil, cover and simmer for 45 minutes, until the mixture has thickened, stirring occasionally. Remove from the heat.

2 Drain and rinse the kidney beans under cold water. Add to the pan with the garlic and season to taste with salt and pepper. Set aside to cool.

3 Place the pizza base on a hot baking sheet and spoon over the chilli mixture. Sprinkle with the cheeses and bake in a preheated oven, 220°C, (425°F), Gas Mark 7, for 15–20 minutes, or according to the pizza base instructions. Serve hot.

2 tablespoons vegetable oil

4 shallots, chopped

1 teaspoon chilli powder

250 g (8 oz) minced beef

225 g (7½ oz) can tomatoes

dash of Tabasco sauce

200 g (7 oz) can red kidney beans

1 garlic clove, crushed

1 ready-made 25 cm (10 inch) pizza base

125 g (4 oz) mozzarella cheese, diced

2 teaspoons grated Parmesan cheese

salt and pepper

Serves 4

Preparation time: 10 minutes, plus cooling

Cooking time: about 1¼ hours

25 g (1 oz) butter

2 onions, sliced

1 ready-made 25 cm (10 inch) pizza base

2–3 green chillies, deseeded and sliced lengthways

1 tablespoon chopped thyme

1 tablespoon chopped marjoram

50 g (2 oz) mozzarella cheese, diced

marjoram sprigs, to garnish

Tomato Sauce:

1–2 tablespoons vegetable oil

1 garlic clove, crushed

2–3 shallots, chopped

250 g (8 oz) tomatoes, finely chopped

150 ml (¼ pint) dry white wine

1 teaspoon dried mixed Italian herbs

salt and pepper

Serves 4

Preparation time: 10 minutes, plus cooling

Cooking time: about 1 hour

1   First make the tomato sauce. Heat the oil in a saucepan, add the garlic and shallots and cook for about 5 minutes, until golden. Add the tomatoes, wine and mixed herbs. Bring to the boil and cook over a low heat for 20 minutes, until thickened. Season to taste with salt and pepper and set aside to cool.

2   Melt the butter in a pan, add the onions and cook for 5 minutes, until golden. Set aside to cool.

3   Put the pizza base on to a hot baking sheet. Spread the onions on the base and cover with the tomato sauce. Sprinkle with the chillies, thyme, marjoram and cheese.

4   Bake in a preheated oven, 220°C, (425°F), Gas Mark 7, for 15–20 minutes, or according to the pizza base instructions. Garnish with the marjoram sprigs and serve hot.

spicy hot pizza

96

index

balti courgettes 76
balti mixed vegetables 75
beans: black bean chilli 70
   chilli bean & pepper soup 12
   chilli bean dip 25
   chilli con carne 59
   kidney bean curry 77
beef: chilli con carne 59
   chilli stir-fry with steak 58
   Chinese beef cappellini 89
   Mexican beef with lime rice 60
biryani, vegetable 80

cabbage: spiced coleslaw 71
Calabrian sauce, pasta with 85
cauliflower, coriander & coconut soup 14
cheese: chillies rellenos 18
   polenta salad with goats' cheese & chilli oil 16
   spicy nachos with cheese 19
Chiang Mai noodles 78
chicken: chicken jalfrezi 46
   curried chicken salad 42
   devilled chicken 50
   gado gado with chicken 43
   grilled chicken Creole 48
   Kashmiri chicken 44
   peppery chicken with pasta 88
   Phuket chicken curry 49
   spiced chicken wings & pepper dip 52
   spicy pot roast chicken 51
   Trinidadian pilau 47
chilli con carne 59
chilli-topped pizza 94
chillied fish 30
chillies 6
   chilli bean & pepper soup 12
   chilli bean dip 25
   chilli stir-fry with steak 58
   chilli oil 9
   chilli pork 64
   chillies rellenos 18
   chillies stuffed with curried crab 28
   salsa cruda 9
   spicy hot pizza 95
Chinese beef cappellini 89
coleslaw, spiced 71
coley: spicy fish cakes 38
courgettes, balti 76
crab: chillies stuffed with curried crab 28
Creole prawns 36
curries: curried chicken salad 42
   fish curry 31
   kidney bean curry 77
   Phuket chicken curry 49
   Thai red curry paste 8
   vegetable curry 81

fajitas, vegetable 74
fettuccine with spicy tomato sauce 86
fish 27–39
fish cakes, spicy 38
fish curry 31
focaccia pizza with pepperoni 93

gado gado with chicken 43

Indian meatballs with tomato curry sauce 90–1

Kashmiri chicken 44

lamb: Indian meatballs 90–1
   lamb casserole with roasted garlic & chilli 62

meat 55–67
meat-stuffed tortillas 56
Mexican beef with lime rice 60
Mexican soup with avocado salsa 15
monkfish: spicy fish stew 32
mustard 6

nachos with cheese 19
noodles, Chiang Mai 78

pakora 22
pasta 84–92
peanut dressing, spicy 8
penne all'arrabbiata 92
peppercorns 6–7
peppers: piperade 24
   stuffed green peppers 23
   vegetable fajitas 74
Phuket chicken curry 49
pilau, Trinidadian 47
piperade 24
pizzas 93–5
polenta salad with goats' cheese & chilli oil 16
pork: chilli pork 64
   meat-stuffed tortillas 56
   sweet & spicy pork 66
potatoes: griddled sausages & mustard mash 65
   spicy potatoes 72
prawns: Creole prawns 36
   prawns & noodles in spicy broth 29
   roasted Thai-style prawns 34
   stir-fried prawns with cumin & chilli 33

rice: Trinidadian pilau 47
   vegetable biryani 80

salads 16–17, 42–3
salsa cruda 9
samosas, vegetable 20
sandwich, red hot turkey 53
sausages: chorizo kebabs 63
   griddled sausages & mustard mash 65
scallops: spicy fish stew 32
sea bass: spicy baked fish 37
soups 12–15
spices 6–7

tagliatelle with chilli balsamic sauce 84
Thai red curry paste 8
tomatoes: fettuccine with spicy tomato sauce 86
   piperade 24
   salsa cruda 9
tortillas, meat-stuffed 56
Trinidadian pilau 47
turkey sandwich, red hot 53

vegetables 69–81
   balti mixed vegetables 75
   pakora 22
   vegetable biryani 80
   vegetable curry 81
   vegetable samosas 20

watercress & pomegranate salad 17